THE POWER OF IDENTITY

7 STEPS TO OVERTAKE AND DOMINATE

MWALE HENRY

COPYRIGHT

LAPTOP LIFESTYLE, LLC

ISBN: 978-0-9864165-1-4

"If you can control a man's thinking you do not have to worry about his action. When you determine what a man shall think you do not have to concern yourself about what he will do. If you make a man feel that he is inferior, you do not have to compel him to accept an inferior status, for he will seek it himself. If you make a man think that he is justly an outcast, you do not have to order him to the back door. He will go without being told; and if there is no back door, his very nature will demand one."

— Carter G. Woodson,
The Mis-Education of the Negro

TABLE OF CONTENTS

DEDICATION

I dedicate this book to my mother, my friend. Her wisdom is beyond any corporate boardroom and her insights are far beyond the concerns of life. Mom, your ability to see things for what they are and your understanding of people for who they are and who they will become is indeed a blessing. I will never forget one of your sayings from my childhood: "when you can see something in the day, don't play foolish and light a candle to try and find it in the night."

To my father, brothers and sisters: our experiences have forged life experiences that have made me stronger, and my love towards you all has grown deeper.

To all my friends, mentors, and new "family" I have discovered across the oceans, I say thank you. Notwithstanding, to my confidant and friend, to you I owe a deep gratitude which words cannot express; special mention will not suffice, but a deep devotion will always exist between us.

A WORD FROM THE AUTHOR

L et me start with three key statements that will help you understand the mission and purpose of this book. First, you already know everything in this book. The mere fact you are reading this means that we share a common interest and a desire to grow and become more than we are. The words that fill these pages are common sense but not common practice. These words are part of us as we both share the same value system. What I attempt to do is to lay this all before you for a final look.

Second, you may have already read everything I have written before: in a book, article, blog or maybe even a greeting card. However, for information to move from short-term into long-term memory, constant repetition can be of great value especially when presented in a different format. When dark days come, which they will, your mind will be able to easily recall these principles—principles with which you have already found an affinity.

Finally, I do not want you to agree with what lies within these pages, nor do I want you to believe me. You already know where you are in your life, and only you can finally assess where you need to be. However, I can tell you that I have painstakingly used these Seven Steps, and they have worked for me. If you will consider them, practice them and monitor your development, you will soon realize the value of these Seven Steps.

My faith speaks through these pages; Christ breathes through each line. These are my experiences recorded in the book of my life. The decision to write this book was born on a Friday night in Calgary, Canada, when I attended a men's prayer meeting before attending a birthday party. You will admit prayer and party are an odd mix, but these apparent contradictions have provided the creative synergy that has inspired me.

I humbly suggest that as you ponder over the words you are about to read, you will realize that the power to become lies with personal revelation and inner convictions.

As you read this book, it is my hope that you will gain a greater desire to live the life you are designed to live. As you reflect on these chapters, you will recognize that the journey of identity and personal discovery lies within your reach. Once you have a glimpse of these possibilities, do not forget this, dreams come with many challenges. It is at this stage you must focus on your goal and not the process. The process can be slow, but the goal inspires you into momentum.

INTRODUCTION

You face constant competition for your attention. Each voice that you hear promotes itself with its own list of priorities, images and beliefs. These voices attempt to tell you who you are, who you are to become or even who you should be. Our struggle for identity is born out of a desire to make sense of the noise around us and to seek certainty in our personal lives. This certainty is either found in simply accepting the identity presented by the loudest voice or by following the calm still voice that says this is the way, walk ye therein.

We must remember that in this fight for identity, there are those who constantly see who you are becoming, judges who determine who lives and who dies. It is a certainty that during your struggle the empty and hungry people, who are starving from within, are the ones who are seeking to destroy you from without. Know those who are empty and those who are full; pay the empty vessels no mind, for you know that empty vessels usually make the most noise.

I am just a simple young man, facing many struggles and changes, and have experienced many watershed moments. All of my experiences, both positive and negative, have assisted me in understanding who I was in that moment, who I was in the past and who I believe I am becoming. Simply by default, life exposes you to many realities and demands. All in all, the decisions that you make reflect the quality of the life that you have now. The responsibility rests upon us to determine our future and to forge a new destiny at every crossroad. We can forge a new pathway at every dead-end street we meet, or we can give into the voices that will suffocate us into stasis and inaction.

Your identity is formulated by your belief system. You either believe something or you don't. Belief drives your actions, and these actions shape your daily activities and your destiny. In Stephen Covey's *Seven Habits of Highly Effective People*, the author prescribes the following key to self-discovery: "Sow a thought, reap a deed, sow a deed, reap a habit, sow a habit reap a lifestyle, sow a lifestyle reap a destiny." Self-identifying, self-reflecting and self-believing thoughts govern our actions. As sure as night follows day, seed, time and harvest will always endure; whatever a man or woman sows, he or she will reap. In the unseen fields of our lives, we find that seed-time and harvest-time are both eternal and tangible.

Our previous thoughts and actions determine what we will become. If we do not think ahead, we will reap few rewards. However, if we act and think wisely, we will reap great rewards and truly be prepared for the future. There is one choice. This is simply a law of life. We truly are what we think and do. We can choose to be the wise, prudent planner or the lazy, short-sighted beggar. Therefore, be careful what you think, because your thoughts run your life. Proverbs 4:23 NCV

Step 1

Create your Vision

"The only thing worse than being blind is having sight, but no vision."

—Helen Keller

The inspiring stories of people who are disabled, but yet have been able to accomplish many tasks and dreams are truly amazing. What is the key ingredient that makes success possible against great odds? Some may say it is determination, passion, consistency or even belief. However the disabled individual, above all the aforementioned qualities, has decided to accept their realities and make them a regular part of their journey. The choice to accept these realties is fundamental to overcoming obstacles and mustering the strength you need to succeed.

Many people in the world have overcome great adversity to make something of themselves. For example, one woman who was severely injured in the 2013 Boston Marathon bombing would not let anything stop her. After countless surgeries and much pain, she finally decided to amputate the leg that was creating so much discomfort and immobility. Before she made that decision, she married the love of her life, who had also suffered injuries on that fateful April day. Her goal is to run in the 2015 Boston Marathon with her prosthetic leg. She wrote recently, "I spent too many years of my life trying to fit in, to blend, to be like everyone else. Now I'm just happy being me. Half a leg less, but getting a lot smarter every day. Each of us is uniquely and perfectly made. Join me in not only embracing . . . but truly CELEBRATING that." Her attitude should inspire us when facing challenges, great or small. The woman's name is Rebekah Gregory, and she represents all of us. We should have a vision in the midst of all of our difficulties.

In the midst of such a challenge there is acceptance. When we accept a challenge, it takes on a life of its own and becomes a part of our lives. Therefore embrace your challenge, as it will take the sting out of the wound and blunt the effects of your pain. Always remember the first stage of healing is to acknowledge and accept the challenge.

> *When we accept a challenge, it takes on a life of its own...*

When you have embraced this truth, you no longer feel as though you have lost something. You have hope like Rebekah Gregory, like so many of those who suffered in the wars, like so many who were born with difficulties. Everyone is of value and everyone can create a future for themselves with the right attitude and motivation.

> *Embrace your challenge, as it will take the sting out of the wound and blunt the effects of your pain.*

A similar mindset looks at a beaten-down economy and sees opportunities. A fired person sees a new job or business on the horizon, not seeing himself as unemployed, but in transition. Even in politics, a candidate or party who has lost an election sees defeat as a moment to reflect and re-tool. Every moment is laced with the opportunity to see things differently and to take responsibility for your future.

Vision causes one to see the possibility in the impossible. During my first trip to Canada, I was leaving my family, close friends and connections; all I had was a possible opportunity. Yes, it was the first time outside of the Caribbean for me—an opportunity to study abroad for one year of my Masters of Philosophy/Ph.D. program as a visiting researcher. Though there were risks, I looked at that year as an opportunity. When the invitation to apply for study abroad had arrived at my home I had thought, "Maybe I should apply; I might just be chosen."

But the due date for the application had passed two days earlier! As I was about to give up on the application, I saw myself in Canada. The possibility became as real to me as though I were actually there.

The seed was planted during the welcoming speech given by the principal of the University of the West Indies, Dr. Tewarie, who spoke of the need for students to have local, regional and international experiences to develop our nation. Seven years later, I was on a plane headed to Calgary, Canada. Seven years later I met the woman of my dreams at a business conference I attended on my way to Canada. The power of vision can create a future that does not currently exist if you never allow that vision to die.

Dr. Steve Maraboli, an inspirational speaker and behavior science coach, said, "we can't undo a single thing we have ever done, but we can make decisions today that propel us to the life we want and toward the healing we need." His book, *Life, the Truth, and Being Free* can motivate people struggling with challenges to set a vision for a life that can help them heal and succeed.

It is true; vision allows you to create the person you want to become. See the future and act as though it is the present. Failure to do so is to resign your dreams to death. In Proverbs 29:18 we are told, "Where there is no vision my people perish." The cost of blindness is destruction. What a tragedy it would have been had I not taken the opportunity presented to me. United States President John Quincy Adams stated, "Patience and perseverance have a magical effect before which difficulties disappear and obstacles vanish." If you cultivate a vision and persevere at it, you will reap fruitful results and your challenges will disappear.

Don't make a list of things you want to get done,
yet decide on who you want to become

Step 2

Cultivate your Vision

"Nothing is more powerful than an idea whose time has come."

—Victor Hugo

If you want to see an idea through to its fulfillment, you must cultivate that idea. Every seed needs nurturing and protecting. You can't simply plant a seed and walk away. Work must be done to ensure that what you have envisioned comes to pass. A farmer knows that what he has planted will not grow simply because he wants it to. Similarly, your vision, your dream will not simply grow because of your burning desire. There is a process you must commit yourself to in order to see a harvest, to see your dreams come to a reality.

Protect Your Vision
It's important to protect your vision by only exposing it to like-minded people. Your vision is something unseen but

inspired, and only those with a similar mind-set will see what you see and feel what you feel. You are not being arrogant when you know for certain the idea which stirs within you is a God-idea.

What is a God-idea? A God-idea is an idea that is bigger than you are; it is so huge that your body shakes at the idea of possessing it. It is so important that it can't be ignored, so inspiring that you walk towards it unconsciously. Follow your passion, because if God ordained your vision, nothing can stop it from coming true.

Do you remember sharing an idea with someone who tried to talk you out of it? Or someone who had something negative to say? Have you ever heard any of these killer phrases? "I don't see how that could work." "I hope you know what you are doing." "Are you sure it's possible?" Sometimes these statements are legitimate and are coming from people who can help to stimulate your critical thinking as a way of improving your vision. However, sometimes these voices come from fear and doubt. These are the individuals you need to be aware of, for their words may plant seeds of doubt in you that may undermine your vision. Remember, "if you are persistent, you will get it. If you are consistent, you will keep it." Don't give up!

Develop your Abilities

I began this chapter about vision with the words of Helen Keller, who although blind, had vision. But there are other kinds of blindness that are not physical, or come from impairment, disadvantages or loss. However, through various struggles, your other senses sharpen because your struggle has become a matter of survival.

Science has shown that in the animal kingdom what a species may lack in one area, their biological nature has compensated for it in another area. For instance, bats are nocturnal creatures, but cannot see at night. However, they have an amplified

---

sense of hearing that allows them to navigate at night using sound as a radar.

Whether or not you like bats, the lesson is clear. In "blindness," there is still a way to see. Our personal deficiencies may have forced us to develop our strengths in other areas of our lives. Therefore, even in "blindness" we see more than ever and we know more than ever.

You know the common saying that the "most talented people are usually the laziest." Many young people who have found themselves before the courts, and are being filtered through our Justice system, have been found to be very innovative in structuring organized crime, leading international trafficking operations, some even engineer or re-engineer arms and ammunition for criminal use. If only their talents were used for legitimate business activities, innovation and community leadership; the world would be a different place. Tragically, they have never seen their potential fully utilized.

Be Innovative

We cannot resign ourselves to the excuse that we have an apparent "weakness." This is not enough. Sometimes we truly learn to do more with less. During this process of self-discovery, we realize that we have the adaptive strength to get us from one point to the other as a matter of survival. We have an opportunity to bless someone else with our dormant, innate gift, a gift that is yet to be discovered.

Let me explain this further. The same bat, which has adapted to survive through "echolocation" is now giving life to someone else. Science has discovered a chemical in their saliva used during feeding that

> *During this process of self-discovery we realize that we have the adaptive strength to get us from one point to the other as a matter of survival.*

contains anticoagulant properties that dissolve blood clots three times faster than regular medicine. Ohio State University has conducted preliminary work in this area and is excited by the promising results - a gift to heart patients and humanity at large.

Just like the bat, your "blindness" heightens your other senses, allowing you do more with less. However, realize that your ability to get things done is not simply for yourself. Your very existence in the race of life can unconsciously provide a lifeline for someone else. Take the time to figure out what may seem natural to you, but to others is producing a positive unintentional impact. Discover what that impact is, and start to be intentional. Your innovative ability should not simply be for a self-fulfilling purpose.

Your very existence in the race of life can unconsciously provide a lifeline for someone else.

Step 3

Never Compete

"Champions never compete they simply win."

—Coach Mwale

When I was growing up with my brothers and sisters, they were always teasing and taunting me, saying "Mwale, you hate to lose!" And they were right; whatever it is, I'm always looking to dominate. However, I always felt some frustration because I was too often focusing on the progress of someone else rather than developing my own personal talents.

Think about this. I remember going to Summer Camp in Trinidad. School was out, and I was a Cub Scout, proud of my green shirt, my hat and my badges. In this one particular race, which I was determined to win, I glanced back at my friend. In that split second, not realizing someone carelessly stepped on to the track—bam! We collided, and I tumbled several times before coming to a face-grinding halt.

I was not OK. It was not the shame, nor the laughter, but the feeling in my right leg. The knee of the other guy had slammed into my thigh. Trust me, at eight years old you think, "That's it. I'm going to die; I'm going to lose my leg!"

The camp counselor ran to my aid, saying, "Why were you not looking ahead?"

"I saw him, but it was too late."

Simply put, I had not been focusing on the race. I learned from that experience that whenever I do anything, I need to focus. I definitely learned from that mistake, just as you can from yours. Mistakes can have a vital impact on us. President Bill Clinton said, "if you live long enough, you'll make mistakes. But if you learn from them, you'll be a better person. The main thing is never quit, never quit."

Pay Attention

Am I aware of others and my environment? Yes!

Am I focused on all I am aware of? No!

Whenever you compete, it is easy to become aware of others while becoming less aware of yourself. The mere fact you can see them alongside you means that you are not focused on your mission. You are losing time and momentum. Therefore, why be distracted? We must always remain focused on our goals. Remember that many of the times we allow ourselves to be distracted by our peers we are actually falling behind.

However, do not forget that your peers are also your competitors.

Make no mistake: though you may be on the same journey, be prepared for a lack of cooperation. Whenever you are aware of this, or even sense this, trust your instinct and quietly remove yourself from that relationship, which can only become a distraction. Distraction does three things:

1. It slows your momentum
2. It moves you away from your goals (you become goal-less)
3. It moves you closer to someone's goal (you become an imitation)

Focusing on your goal allows you to build momentum. The greatest tragedy in a society driven on consumption and not production and personal innovation is that too many people take signals from others as to what is important. Too many of us are guilty of comparing ourselves to others and neglecting the treasure of our own lives.

John Maxwell teaches in his *Five Levels of Leadership* that once you focus on building momentum, your problems will begin to correct themselves. Think of a truck driving over a piece of wood two feet high while traveling at seventy miles per hour. Now think of this same truck at a standstill, facing this same two-foot tall piece of wood. Its movement would be greatly impeded. Whenever the smallest thing in life resists or hinders you, your momentum has been lost.

Run your Race

Everyone has unique potential, once discovered and developed, it will bring you victory! The issue will no longer be *if* you will win, but simply *when* will you win. Let's be honest; many people have accepted the role of imitating others, deceiving themselves that they are being original. This is the highest form of personal neglect and self-hate.

> *The issue will no longer be if you will win, but simply when will you win.*

Let me illustrate the importance of walking in your unique potential. In the pre-qualifying javelin throw in the 2012

Olympics, world record holder and Gold medalist Keshorn Walcott of Trinidad and Tobago brought pride to our nation. Among the many reasons for his success were his faith in God, family support, discipline and execution. If you ask anyone involved in high-pressure circumstances, when that pressure comes, your instincts and mental state are the only things that matter. Everything else is instinctive because of excellent training and coaching. Keshorn's mental state gave him the ability to achieve peak performance. His healthy mental state was as a result of him realizing that he was not competing against others. Let's look at the words of his coach, who fostered Keshorn's talents from the beginning:

> The current World Junior champion, who began taking javelin seriously at around sixteen years old, spent three years under Andalcio's tutelage before Cuban coach Ismael Lopez Mastrapa took over. Andalcio was hesitant to predict a medal for the teenager but believes he will improve on his personal best of 82.83 meters in the final. I am extremely proud of him. He's a guy who is strongly motivated and has already achieved everything he has set out to do this year (CAC Junior and World Junior gold medals) so he will be throwing with a free mind. He doesn't have that pressure on him anymore.

Commenting on Walcott's performance in the qualifying round, Andalcio believes nerves played a part in the young athlete's first two throws, which were below eighty meters, before getting it together on his final attempt.

> When I went to Beijing (for the Olympics) in 2008, I came back with video footage of the javelin event. In the prelims on Wednesday he was a little overawed by competing against some of the guys he's been accustomed to seeing, but he is in the final and does not have that "jumbie" over him anymore.

Andalcio explained to *Newsday* that from the very first time he saw Walcott, he realized he was going to be something special.

These words by Keshorn's former coach give us insight on Keshorn's mental philosophy. Any person who begins any major challenge must first begin with three important things:

1. A mindset of accomplishment. The mere fact you are about to engage in a great task means you were successful in the journey to where you are now.

2. You have nothing to prove. You have done it already; this new phase is simply a bonus.

3. Run your own race in the presence of others, but mentally do it alone.

Keshorn knew he had already accomplished what he had set out to do; being in the finals was an accomplishment itself. He had nothing to lose and everything to gain.

This is where your potential will be realized, when you understand that the greatest competition is with yourself. You are the greatest challenge you will ever face.

An African proverb says, "Once we conquer the person within, the enemy without can do us no harm."

> *The greatest competition is with yourself. You are the greatest challenge you will ever face.*

Stay in your Lane

I will be really vulnerable here. Growing up, there was a lot of pressure put on me from friends to succeed. I read many books and was always interested in politics. To my peers, that was boring stuff; they called me an "old man" in a young boy's body.

I accepted that. However, the expectation to succeed was high. If I did not perform at the top of the class, people would wonder what was wrong with me. Now, some of this I brought on myself, because I always liked a challenge and I called for it publicly. However, even when the competition was over, the expectation to win always remained.

Despite this, my school days were good days. I am always happy to see my old school mates in the supermarket or when I meet them at the mall. But sometimes I will meet a former classmate or co-worker who will avoid me when he or she sees me. The awkwardness in their eyes, body language and speech is very apparent, and no matter how much I attempt to be friendly, the tension is still there.

We all know why this is the case. We compare ourselves to each other, and measure our successes based on the jobs we have, the clothes we wear, the cars we drive and the list goes on. Whenever we meet someone who we have started with on this journey called life, we measure ourselves against that person. This is the worst decision you can ever make.

Your gifts, talents and opportunities will always vary; hence you need to be focused and stay in your lane. Only when you focus on your skill-set, will you determine if you are a sprint athlete or a marathon runner. The twist and turns in your life will always be different from other people. Never feel ashamed about where you are. Anyone who is serious knows that success is a journey and not a destination. Therefore the place you are right now is simply temporary; you are in transition. Even if it takes you a while, stay in your lane. Do not give up your right. This is not a race; it is a journey. We will discuss more about the forthcoming steps.

> *Never feel ashamed about where you are. Anyone who is serious knows that success is a journey and not a destination.*

As Harvey MacKay says, "Life is too short to wake up with regrets. So love the people who treat you right. Forget about those who don't. Believe everything happens for a reason. If you get a chance, take it. If it changes your life, let it. Nobody said life would be easy; they just promised it would most likely be worth it."

Step 4

Failure is Just an Opinion

"I've missed more than 9000 shots in my career. I've lost almost 300 games. Twenty-six times, I've been trusted to take the game winning shot and missed. I've failed over and over and over again in my life. And that is why I succeed."

—Michael Jordan

My biggest fear was failure. I say "was" because failure had everything to do with other people and very little to do with me.

I can count on several hands, if you would lend me yours, my list of "failures:" not being able to attend the high school of my choice; failing at a public speaking competition where I represented my school; being fired from one of the most exciting jobs I ever held; not being able to meet personal financial obligations; losing the Guild of Student Elections. The list is long, and failure was real. However, every time I felt rejected, or there was a misstep or a false start I kept hearing in my soul, "failure is only an opinion."

Every time I had these inner conversations, I worried about how people would see me. I don't want to be embarrassed! I don't want to be remembered in the worst way. I can't handle the shame. What are they thinking? Do I have toilet paper stuck to the bottom of my shoes? Is my zipper down? What are they watching?

This is the "shame, fear, control" syndrome, which lead you to do nothing, a paralysis that leads you to never pursue anything new. Don't be afraid to try something new. As the saying goes, "broken things can become blessed things if you let God do the mending."

It is only in action that you can realize who you really are. No activity can only create decay. As the Second Law of Thermodynamics actually proves, life is always in constant decay. Therefore, if you thought by sitting this one out to avoid risk and ensure self-preservation, you are only increasing the rate of your decay. Even a car that is stationary for months will begin to

> *No activity can only create decay.*

decay. Nothing stays new. Therefore it is better to keep your life in constant motion; these activities produce energy and unfold your potential. In fact, making mistakes and experiencing failure are clues that you are in the champion's arena; only fighters can get bruised. Make up your mind to experience failure; those who stay on the sideline simply allow themselves to decay slowly until they are destroyed.

We all make Mistakes

There is no person on earth that has never made a mistake or experienced failure. In fact, history remembers the victories of great men because of their failures. Defying all odds, all eyes are turned to your possible defeat when suddenly you triumph, turning defeat into great victory.

Abraham Lincoln was one the greatest presidents because of his many defeats: several failed attempts at public office, personal bankruptcy and the death of a lover. These "failures" caused him to be a stronger person and ultimately gave him the strength to become president of the United States during the Civil War. If he had not failed, he would not have been motivated to keep trying. If he had not suffered, he would not have been able to relate to those who were losing loved ones in battle. His challenges enabled him to be a successful politician, citizen, friend, husband and father.

Patrick Manning, the former prime minister of Trinidad and Tobago, faced defeat at the national polls twice after he had called for early elections. He fell ill due to the stress of politics and was rejected in the court of public opinion. In contrast, the international community heralds him as a Caribbean leader. Mr. Manning was awarded the "Democracy Prize" by the Guyana Institute for Democracy for his outstanding work in upholding the principles of democracy in the Caribbean. In 2007 he was awarded an honorary Doctor of Letters by Medgar Evers College, an award he accepted on behalf of the people of Trinidad and Tobago. In December 2004, he was awarded the Caribbean Central American Action's "Star of the Caribbean" award. Such international success came at a great cost. The ability of his administration to make unpopular decisions all reaped rewards for the nation of Trinidad and Tobago, years after the decisions were made.

Today Trinidad is a major natural gas-producing country and has one of the largest ammonia plants in the world. Revenues from such successful policy decisions allowed Mr. Manning's administration to create the Heritage and Stabilization Fund, a fund designed to create over twelve months of emergency funding in the event of a global financial crisis. In addition, his flagship decision to provide free education at all levels - including college, for citizens of

Trinidad and Tobago is the true measure of his success. He had the power to make selfless contributions amidst all odds and personal loss.

Another example of defying all odds comes from inventor Lewis H. Latimer. Thomas Edison conducted over eighty experiments until he was able to create the electric light bulb. However, it was Lewis H. Latimer who created the carbon filament, which allowed Edison's light bulb to display light for longer hours, making it practical for lighting in homes and streets. This black scientist developed the technology that made Edison's rediscovery of the electric light bulb a success.

Neither Manning nor Latimer was afraid of failure, because their mistakes allowed them to grow. According to Steve Maraboli, "we all make mistakes, have struggles, and even regret things in our past. But you are not your mistakes, you are not your struggles, and you are here NOW with the power to shape your day and your future."

Victories make us Happy, but Failures make us Sharper

No guts, no glory, no pain no story. Modern society has made us consumers and not producers. The capitalist model has brought focus on the main qualities that create a great customer service experience:

1. Convenience

2. Speed and efficiency

3. Pleasure

4. Cost effectiveness

Very few people see the necessity for self-identity because they would rather watch a championship fight than become a champion themselves. To be a champion requires the following:

High inconveniences. Speak to any leader and they will tell you their greatest opportunities came at the greatest times of inconveniences. Their personal plans had to be changed because of unforeseen circumstances. When this decision is made, it may seem to take you away from your most ambitious dreams; however, your greatest significance lies in choosing self-sacrifice. Nelson Mandela's life is a testament of this. His choice to fight for equality in South Africa caused him to be imprisoned for twenty-seven years, but he overcame and became the President of South Africa. Many would point to his imprisonment as his sacrifice. However, his greatest sacrifice actually began when he decided to abandon his father's desire for him to become a tribal leader. He ran away to Johannesburg, completed his law degree and became one of the few "privileged" black lawyers. However, he abandoned this privileged professional career and joined the struggle for a free South Africa. The call to serve often comes at the most inopportune time. This is a sign.

A slow but consistent journey. Nothing great comes quickly. That's why diamonds are precious; they endure pressure over a long period of time. We need time to learn from our mistakes, time to recover, time to heal, time to learn endurance, time to cry. As Harvey MacKay says, "time is free, but it's priceless. You can't own it but you can use it. You can't keep it but you can spend it. Once you've lost it you can never get it back," so use it wisely.

Pain. The absence of pain makes life boring. Yes, I said it! Pain is a functional part of life, which allows us to define what joy is and what victory tastes like. Pain stimulates gratitude, reconnects us to our humanity and points out

> *The absence of pain makes life boring.*

the necessity for the eternal and the divine. The people who suffer the most are the people who desire pain free lives. The more pleasure and happiness are pursued as an end in themselves, the more vices are created. Morality becomes amoral, relative and exploratory. The concept of family life changes and matrimony is questioned, fidelity becomes optional, parenthood is diluted simply because economic power has become synonymous with pleasure. Do not allow your life story to be about

> *Remember, victories bring joy but failures make us sharper.*

the pursuit of happiness. This is a façade… let it be the pursuit of purpose. These lessons will be an inheritance for your generation. Remember, victories bring joy but failures make us sharper.

High Cost. Greatness never goes on sale. I have never forgotten that statement since I first heard it from Bishop T. D. Jakes. It had me thinking. Anything of great quality is never cheap.

There is always a price tag on any highly valued item. It can be Christmas, Cyber Monday, Black Friday, Thanksgiving or New Years, yet only the low quality items in every store will be truly discounted. However, the price of premier products hold their value. Do not drag your life down to the bargain basement. The old Chinese proverb rings in my ear: "Good things no cheap and cheap things no good."

Pay the full price to meet your goals. Success is going to take long nights, losing some friends, isolation, personal investment, prayer and constant, positive affirmations. Please consider that in most cases high prices mean high quality and high quality lasts. I prefer long lasting wins to short-term gains, which will always cost more in the long run.

Never be afraid to hear the word NO! We all are afraid of rejection. Therefore, we hedge our bets. If we believe there is a high probability of success we move forward; however, if we think the odds are not in our favor, we hesitate. What a mental trap! Re-read this paragraph and tell me what you really think.

Did you read it again? If not, please do.

Human nature is already predisposed to think negatively. On any matter, we are more eager to believe a lie than the truth.

We are also predisposed to believe a rumor. We doubt, we critique, we cast aspersions, we murmur, we praise others briefly, we argue at length; many are simply filled with apathy. There is little hope or trust in humanity.

We have all done this. Yet my question remains: why are you hiding behind the fact that you are basing your actions on approval from others? Do you not realize this is a failed strategy?

Let us consider this. You want to attend an important conference, as it has direct application to your career. With great enthusiasm, you have made up in your mind that you want to go. However, you need the approval from your supervisor. Immediately you begin to wonder. Would the company approve? Is my supervisor in a good mood? I do not think I will receive approval. They never sent anyone before.

In this process, you have talked yourself out of even asking to go to the conference. You have deceived yourself into believing your choice is a result of an expected response from someone you have not even spoken to. Let's put this into perspective.

Nothing is wrong with hearing NO!

I hear it a lot of times. However, I remember listening to a direct sales marketer who once said that it is better to hear NO,

---

so you can get closer to your YES. If your supervisor says no, you can always go over his or her head. Be bold but respectful in asking for what you want. No one in life is sitting around wondering how he or she can help you.

In your preparation for the NOs in life, you must never allow important plans to rest solely in the hands of others. Contingency plans will allow you to navigate through your NOs. I have learned to plan for the worst while hoping for the best. However, while moving thorough your plans, do not lose your sense of zeal. Winston Churchill, who is known for his persistence and nerves of steel, says "success is moving from failure to failure without losing your enthusiasm."

It took me three attempts to get my driver's license. Three times. The first time, my feet trembled so much on the clutch it was like a

> *You must never allow important plans in the hands of others.*

rhythm section in a band. The second time, I did fine, only to learn that the officer who supervised the test wanted a bribe to give me a passing grade, which I declined. The third time, a similar request was implicitly made, and I refused again. To my surprise, the supervisor passed me without receiving a bribe.

I smile when I hear the word NO from someone! It activates my contingency plan and excludes others from my equation for success. You will realize even in business, amateurs convince, and professionals sift and sort. Do not try to convince someone against their will to be a part of your vision. Conserve your energy for your goal, as you will need it.

> *I smile when I hear the word NO from someone! It activates my contingency plan and excludes others from my equation for success.*

I remember hearing the story of a guy who failed his bar examination 47 times. He finally passed on the 48th try. Can you imagine the kind of mockery and scorn he must have faced before his final success? He might have been known as the lawyer who truly "raised the bar" in his pursuit of becoming a practicing lawyer. In the final analysis, he passed. That is all that matters. He did it.

Here is an action plan to deal with NO:

1. Never be emotionally attached to someone's final response.

2. Keep a healthy distance between your request and the answer.

3. Plan for your NO and you will prepare for your YES.

Step 5

Have the Right Perspective

"Oh Lord Bless me indeed and enlarge my territory.
That your hand would be unto me and that you will keep
me from evil. And the Lord granted him that which he
requested."

—1 Chronicles 4:10

In this chapter I want to address the power of perspective, one of the seven steps that are necessary to overtake and dominate. I opened with the historical account of a man named Jabez, who was faced with a family lineage of people who simply lived and died. However when his turn came, he changed his perspective and redefined the outcome of his life and chose to be named among the significant. I was reminded of a story about a girl from Maryland who learned this lesson when she was first learning to drive. While learning, she was so anxious that she would only look directly in front of her so as not to hit anything. However, her anxiety caused her to miss the broader perspective of oncoming traffic and possible impending danger.

Similarly, in school you will learn specific perspectives about various socio-economic theories. Simply put, everyone has a unique view on the same topic, matter and subject; however, where you choose to cast your eyes is exactly what you will see.

The idea that a glass is either half empty or half full is not just a perspective, but an attitude towards life. Whatever your perception, it will determine how you interpret the facts of your life. You must always be willing to see your life free from the emotions of fear and anxiety.

For instance, I once stood near a friend's iMAC computer and was pouring water from a jug into a bottle, so I could carry it with me for the rest of the day. However, my

> *You must always be willing to see your life free from the emotions of fear and anxiety.*

friend walked in and immediately saw, in his mind, water pouring out of the jug onto his computer. With great anguish he ran to his desk, only to realize I was actually standing two feet away from his computer. From his vantage point all he could see was me ruining his computer. At times, your perspective will present false realities. Allow your worldview to be flexible enough to receive new information before you form a myopic conclusion.

Broaden your Horizons

Take every opportunity to learn. As Jose Marti, a renowned nineteenth century poet from Cuba wrote in the first verse of *A Sincere Man Am I* "I'm a traveller to all parts and a newcomer to none."

Take time to travel, ask questions, and question your answers. Many people are afraid to expose themselves to different ideas. However, as one of the greatest Christian apologists Ravi Zacharias always contends, your faith must be measured and tested. If what you believe must be protected and cannot face scrutiny then it is not faith at all. Therefore, an honest discourse should always be welcomed with wisdom and humility.

I had the unique opportunity to be raised in a home where my parents were of two opposite worlds. My mother is a devoted Pentecostal and my dad is anti-religion. All of my siblings grew up with a foundation of faith in God, but we also grew up with the freedom to choose our own paths. I was able to assess for myself all that life had to offer and to learn from the experiences of my siblings. Because of this, my choice to be a Christian was not a decision taken lightly but was based on exposure to academic, cultural, spiritual and socioeconomic ideas.

Every man must be fully committed to his course of action. One must never be forced upon a path, nor goaded into one. Both my parents were passionate about something. My father loved science, spending over thirty-five years as a petroleum lab technician, and wanted me to study science. The more I studied science the more I liked it.

> *Every man must be fully committed to his course of action.*

However, once I was exposed to the social sciences, I was passionate. Was my father disappointed in my choice? Yes! Did he support my career choice? Somewhat reluctantly. However, I know he was proud when I graduated from college at the top of my class.

What is holding you back from trying something new? Are you just pleasing others while sabotaging your true potential? Whenever we operate from fear and intimidation, we will never discover the true self that lies within.

I never forgot the day when I decided to leave my country for the first time to go on a relief mission to Grenada. My mother was afraid of the possible dangers. Like every mother who loves her last child in a unique way, my decision was very discomforting to her. However, she decided to let me go; I decided to go forward. And it was one of the most life-transforming experiences I have ever had. The friendships formed more than ten years ago have endured. My first visit was so powerful for me that I returned for relief work immediately after the island of Grenada was devastated by Hurricane Ivan.

Accept Rejection

When you decide to broaden your horizons, you will not be liked. A decision to learn more and ask more is a decision of separation. You cannot want more out

> *The decision to seek more, to learn more, is a decision to make your familiar places a strange land.*

of life, while hoping things will remain the same. The decision to seek more, to learn more, is a decision to make your familiar places a strange land.

Therefore, learn the art of accepting the rejection of others. If you are accepted by everyone, most likely you have abandoned or compromised your personal goals because of your need to be accepted. When this happens, your circle of friends and associates are not challenging you enough. T. Harv Ecker's *Secrets of the Millionaire Mind*, discusses some interesting facts about the power of association. You will earn money in direct portion to the friends you associate with and the value you bring to the market place. Your net worth is determined by your network; you will earn within the average of the five people you spend most of your time.

Be around inspiring people, people who challenge you, your faith and your beliefs. It is only when your life is tested that you will know where you stand and what you believe. A sheltered life is a life that cannot be trusted. Your rela-

> *A sheltered life is a life that cannot be trusted.*

tionships must be tested. Only those relationships that have integrity will stand. You will learn that some friendships are not worth keeping, many are seasonal and some will simply fade away.

Never personalize these changes, because not all relationships can continue. This is simply a fact. The nature of every relationship will change. Your friends from high school and college have changed because their lives have changed. Yet there are some relationships that no matter how long or far apart you may be from each other, whenever you do connect, it feels like you have never missed a moment. These are relationships that are few and far between. Whenever they happen to you, cherish and nurture them.

Never Forget

I take a page out of Jewish history, for the phrase "Never Forget" is used by the Jewish nation to pay homage to what their forefathers had to endure under the gruesome experience of the Holocaust. Every Jew shares one common commitment to: "Never Forget."

The lobbying power of the Jewish community is significant, as Jews seek to protect their interest. A great lesson can be learned from their "Never Forget" mantra.

If you are to dominate, first you must be willing to tell your family's story. If you do not know what it is, find it. If you cannot find it, borrow from someone else. The reality of a story is a narrative of history that provides constant inspiration. We all gain inspiration when we ascribe a hero status to someone based on their great achievements,

> *The reality of a story is a narrative of history that provides constant inspiration.*

from Martin Luther King Jr., Marcus Garvey, Uriah Buzz Butler to Eric Williams. We may have never met these great men, but their story gives us hope today.

In addition, be unified. My mentor once told me that you cannot accomplish anything without unity. You may be able to go faster alone, but you will be able to go further together. Create long-lasting relationships. Seek out partnerships and be intentional; you cannot do it alone. In these partnerships you will be accountable to someone.

Volunteer for a cause greater than yourself. Do not look for anything in return. All partnerships do not necessarily have to be symbiotic. Many great men and women have been in the struggle simply because of the main objective. The struggle was not for money or fame. No one was paid to organize, no incentive was offered.

Many of life's lessons can be learned in the trenches of volunteering. I remember having the privilege to speak with John Maxwell, and he told me that some of our greatest leadership skills are born in places of volunteerism. In fact, he advised every CEO to assess a leader's ability to influence in a setting where influence is not based on tittle, compensation or fear. Once a leader is able to influence someone in such an environment, he is truly a leader.

Learn to serve without expecting to gain something in return. You will be amazed at the heart-filled lessons you will learn. Only when you capture the heart of service, which is your currency of trade, will you earn the lifestyle you desire.

President Barack Obama recognized the value of grassroots service by establishing the Office of Social Innovation and Civic Participation in an attempt to translate the widespread interest of service into sustainable impact. What's more important, companies of all shapes and sizes see employee volunteer programs as valuable and worthwhile, particularly in difficult economic times.

The former president of the Thunderbird School of Global Management, Ángel Cabrera, knows that companies with global ambitions need a workforce—and leadership—to match those ambitions.

Cabrera wrote in his 2012 book, *Being Global*, that the "challenges of global engagement require leaders at the helm who can craft solutions by seamlessly bringing together people and resources across national, cultural, and organizational lines." According to Cabrera, now president of George Mason University, this means companies "can't just act global. They need to be global." Therefore, CEOs who volunteer and encourage employee volunteerism can help spread their business globally as well.

Step 6

Command your Critics

"The trouble with most of us is that we would rather be ruined by praise than saved by criticism."
—Norman Vincent Peale

All criticism is not bad. You need feedback for development. The most important people in your life are those people who tell you things about yourself you do not know. This is the highest form of personal growth: to find out something new about yourself. Allow people to know you and share things with you, aspects of yourself that you may not even be aware of. Once you hear new information about yourself, no matter how bitter it feels, you will know so much more.

In this learning process called discovery, you will realize that you have developed specific habits of which you are not aware. Once you make the necessary changes to eliminate a negative habit, you will change the way people interact with you; you will change the way people respond to you. Productive criticism can help you move from a place of dysfunction into a place of functionality. Think of it this way: before I started track and field at school, our physical education teacher told us to straighten up our backs. After one week, I was standing tall and walking straight. Ever since then, I have walked with a healthier posture, a posture that positively affects the way people interact with me.

> *Productive criticism can help you move from a place of dysfunction into a place of functionality.*

Know that everyone who criticizes also has a critic; hence never allow criticism to reign supreme in your life. Eat the fish, but leave the bones behind. There is something to learn from your critique. You must be able to allow good friends to say tough things to you because they love you. As Sarita Jakes puts it, "it's like allowing a friend to wear something atrocious, while strangers say 'either she doesn't have a mirror or she doesn't have a friend.'

One of the main reasons good leaders fail, sometimes at great cost, is their over sensitivity to criticism. As a leader if you are not willing to listen to criticism, you will not be able to make informed decisions.

I am reminded of the account of the Prophet Elijah, when he prayed for rain, to end a three year drought. He commanded his servant to go and look six times, and each time he reported that he saw nothing. On the seventh time he reported that he saw "a little cloud about the size of a man's hand rising from the sea." Elijah believed that rain would fall, but he insisted that he receive real information about his progress. Let your team tell you the truth; listen to the troops so you can make informed decisions. Always, always leave room for feedback.

You need Actual Data

Allow yourself to be spoken to, rather than speaking to others. It's powerful when someone talks *to* you, rather than *about* you. In fact, it's better at times to let the conversation be one way and allow silence to be your response. You have a moment to practice silence, which is the moment where you give up your right to respond and just listen. It's an opportunity to learn.

Many times you will realize the area of your criticism has nothing to do with you. Failure to listen may cause you to miss an opportunity of realizing that the criticism has nothing to do with you. This is crucial and can be easily missed; on many occasions this has determined the

> *It's better at times to let the conversation be one way and allow silence to be your response.*

difference of being married or divorced, hired or fired or, even worse, living or dying.

Let's consider what you have just read. You may have just started a new relationship and you face a series of criticism that bears no resemblance to you. You know it! You have carefully examined your partner's words and you do not agree with them. To an untrained and quick-tempered person, you may become defensive. However a patient soul takes the time to respond to the 'real' issue and gets to the core of the matter, rather than wasting time on minor matters. In the 39th verse of *I Have a Rose To Tend,* Marti writes about tending a white rose all year and giving it to a true friend. But he also gives one to "the cruel one whose blows break the heart by which I live." In other words, it is even worth cherishing criticism that you believe at the moment may be incorrect.

You may have experienced undue scrutiny from your supervisor, as it relates to your work assignments. However, at times, the source of this pressure is actually coming from your supervisor's superiors. Once you realize this, you know giving a brief response is critical in that moment. Frequently the best response is to simply say nothing.

Suffer Well

Yes, I said it! Suffer like a boss under criticism; especially under the unfair punches that will come your way. You are not worth your metal or muscle if you have not been unfairly criticized, especially by those closest to you. You will sometimes get painful criticism from friends and family. However, through your persecution you earn the right to be heard because of the things you have suffered.

Les Brown says that "life will hit you on the blind side; and when you get knocked down be sure to land on your back, because once you can look up, you

> ℘
>
> *Suffer like a boss under criticism; especially under the unfair punches that will come your way.*

can get up." Learn to receive a good licking and keep on ticking. To do so, you must be able to thrive under pressure. The more life squeezes you, the more you will discover the work you have to do.

In addition, under pressure, life will test the quality of your friendships. Only in a crisis you will know who your friends are. Friendship has to do with commitment—through thick or thin, right or wrong. Friendships like the one I am describing are few and far between. In your pursuit to be a part of something greater, I encourage you think about your friends and pray for tragedy, because the sooner you face difficulties the sooner you will know who your friends really are.

Storms will come, but I would much rather be surrounded with a friend in a storm than a crowd in the sun or alone in the rain. Criticism from others is a great testing ground before the real war.

Therefore, suffer well under criticism. This will require a level of faith and belief; it will not be easy, but it is necessary. However, it is equally necessary for criticism to happen as it is for it to stop. Here are some tips that will help you to endure:

1. Persist when nothing is happening

2. Remain focused when everyone is ignoring you

3. Remain faithful when celebrated

4. Increase your commitment when you are not celebrated

5. See betrayal as a blessing

Fine-tune your Focus

Apart from suffering well, fine-tune your focus. I have a friend who told me once that I have a 'gift' of ignoring people. I almost did not hear her. This statement came while she was hurling insults at me, which I refused to hear. Yes, we became friends eventually, and I am not using the word "friend" loosely.

To remain focused you need to re-tune your frequency. To re-tune means you were once focused and now you are not. Negative criticism to me is like unwanted and interrupted noise on the radio. When I was a child, our old radio had no digital dial. To locate a particular radio station was a skill, executed with great precision, so the dial could be tuned by hand to the correct station.

However, at times we would lose the signal entirely, depending on the signal's strength, weather patterns and other circumstances beyond our control. Sometimes the signal was lost, sometimes interrupted by a Spanish radio broadcast from Venezuela. As a child, we often said that if someone kept interrupting a conversation, he or she was butting-in like a Spanish radio station.

The solution to this was to fine-tune the dial by hand so we would be able to hear with great clarity our desired station. All of the static and interruption would be gone.

Likewise, you must tune out critical voices, which simply act as interruptions and do not provide solutions. Alter your inner negative conversations by reading good books and listening to good music. Share your heart with your mentor, because seeking good advice to troubling situations is virtuous.

Have different types of friends

As previously mentioned, friendships are important if you wish to overtake and dominate. However, understanding the types of friendships you foster and maintain is essential. There are three main types of friendships; serious, casual and task specific friendships. Serious friends are people with whom you discuss life-changing issues and from whom you seek advice. These are important friends to have.

Casual friends are those with whom you may have important conversations, but in no great detail. These people are important to you based on your history and former relationships. However, you know these friends do not have the required experience or expertise to advise you because your life is simply going in a different direction and you have changed over the course of your relationship with them. But because of familiar ties, you maintain these relationships because you genuinely care about them.

Task specific friends are your gym buddies, sparring partners, walking buddies—you come together for a specific task.

When that event has ended, you will see each other again the next time. This type of relationship is maintained through extremely light conversations; you discuss nothing heavy, lengthy or personal about your life with them. You admire them for their skills in a specific area, and you enjoy their light-hearted company.

Once you learn to navigate these types of friendships in different aspects of your life, you will have the mental ease you need to deal with the greater issues of life. You can do it!

Step 7

Forgive or be Forgotten

Bear with each other and forgive one another
if any of you has a grievance against
someone. Forgive as the Lord
forgave you.

—Colossians 3:13-15

I decided to leave the topic of forgiveness for my last chapter, because it is the most fundamental key to your ability to overtake and dominate. If you fail to forgive, you are carrying a person on your back. Your progress will be slow or non-existent, especially if you have more than one person whom you refuse to forgive.

I have known many otherwise great, talented people with great potential, but who simply lacked the ability to forgive. They have lost everything as a result. Above all else, do not neglect this key called forgiveness. The decision not to forgive is like deciding to drink poison and expecting your offender to die.

Forgiveness is a liberating experience. It brings a sense of relief from the past that one can never anticipate. It keeps you grounded in the present, while your decision to let go builds for you a better future. Many people have the misconception that the person whom the grudge is held against is the unfortunate one. On the contrary, the person holding the grudge is the one who is trapped in negative feelings. The one holding the grudge is the one who is at risk for sleepless nights and psychological torment, even leading to physical illness.

I know that it is difficult to move forward and free yourself from the inner strife and bitterness you feel towards someone who has wronged you.

The three strategies for forgiveness that I want to share with you will guide your process of forgiveness. It is a process that will take some time. However, let the process start, and give yourself the freedom you deserve.

Forgiveness is the Launching Pad to your Future

Every time you are offended, see it as an opportunity to launch into your future. See forgiveness as an opportunity to be light-hearted and to become free. The liberating freedom you feel when you choose to forgive is an essential ingredient for your success. Practice forgiveness immediately after the offense occurs. Forgiving is easier to do when it is done in the moment.

You might say that it is harder to forgive in the moment; however, the greatest time to gain momentum is in the moment. This is

> *Practice forgiveness immediately after the offense occurs.*

similar to launching yourself off a diving board. The longer you stay on the board, the harder it is to jump.

You may have heard of Corrie ten Boom, the author of *The Hiding Place*. She and other members of her family helped many Jews escape from the Netherlands during World War II. For this, she was held in a concentration camp for almost a year and was only released on a technical error. For years after she was released, she'd have nightmares and wake up remembering the horrors of her experience. She started speaking to people everywhere, talking about her experiences and her belief in God. One day a man came up to her and thanked her for her speech. She immediately recognized him as one of the SS guards from the camps. She stiffened, and her chest grew tight, as she struggled to forgive him. This was difficult to do, as she remembered all he had done to the women in the camp. She prayed for a right heart, and she was able to greet him with a smile and shake his hand as she remembered that one must love one's enemies.

Do not allow your pain to settle, or replay the offense in your subconscious. I remembered when I sky dived for the first time. I told the instructor that when it was time to jump, just go! No delays! Unfortunately, my request was not granted. I stood on the edge of the plane, doors open, strapped to the instructor. I was dangling out, body slamming against the wind, with nothing to hold onto, for approximately twenty seconds before we jumped. Those twenty seconds felt like an hour. With every second that passed, the closer I came to quitting! Once we jumped from 10,000 feet, free falling sixty seconds at 180mph, it was a tremendous thrill that I will do again and again.

The danger was real, the threat of death was real. However, I decided to do it anyway. Similarly, the pain of betrayal and attack is real. You sometimes even want revenge, but forgive anyway and do it quickly, even when you feel like you are not ready. A decision to start at once gets you closer to your goal of healing. Let your revenge be focused on your God-given assignment on earth. Frank Sinatra puts it best: the best revenge is massive success.

Forgiveness, is Your Instrument of Compassion

One day at church, I was standing in the back as an usher. To my surprise a group of little girls came crying to me, all talking at the same time, lodging their complaints, all in a chorus of tears. After calming them down, I soon realized that it was a fight over a doll and whose turn it was to brush the doll's hair. One of the girls complained that she did not get her turn and the rest of the group suddenly decided they were not going to play with her. I quickly encouraged them all to get along with each other and stop pulling at the doll. Within less than five minutes they were all playing together like nothing had happened.

Learning from the innocence of a child is crucial to our ability to forgive. Do not allow experiences to harden your heart. Children have such a simple faith whatever problems they face, today is the greatest moment they have. They let go of the past as quickly as it happened, and they treat their friends with a heart of innocence. We must all learn to love like a child and forgive as a child. Whenever you have time,

> *Do not allow experiences to harden your heart.*

observe them carefully and you will see their hearts are always free-spirited. All of us were once children; innocent, gullible and carefree.

I will not for a second promote the concept of "forgive and forget." I say "forgive and learn." If you do not learn the pain will return. Gandhi was right: if we live by the slogan "an eye for an eye and a tooth for a tooth, the entire world will be blind, so the only way out is through forgiveness." Martin Luther King Jr. was a huge proponent of forgiveness during the civil rights movement. He said, "that he who is devoid of the power to forgive is devoid of the power to love."

Forgiveness is Your Second Wind

Forgiveness is your second wind, kicking in just before the finish line. Without fail, every time I am about to do something of great importance, someone comes to create problems. Sometimes the act would be very small, but small errors are amplified if you are under pressure. It is important to learn, even if the offense is valid, not to be offended.

An offense may pop up when you are about to reach your goal. Sometimes it is lurking at the finish line, hoping to slow you down. Please note; do not become consumed with the smoke and mirrors of life. Always keep in mind that an offense may be a

> *An offense may be a sign that you are closer to your goal than you actually think.*

sign that you are closer to your goal than you actually think. Forgiveness will come at a time when you need it the most.

Like that athlete who is about to finish his race and gets his second wind which allows him to finish strong, you must find the second wind you need to overcome the burden of un-forgiveness. However, it is not oxygen we need but one deep breath called "forgiveness." Once inhaled, forgiveness is that last push that will take you to your finish line. Remember, failure to forgive is a decision to give up your prize of standing on the podium of victory.

Failure to forgive is a decision to give up your prize of standing on the podium of victory.

Claim your FREE Gift at www.FaithTour.org

CONCLUSION

As I close let me leave you with the following poem by Barry Maltese, titled *Forgiveness*, which summarizes the last step and indeed much of what this book is about.

> If you try to reach inside of your heart
> And from that place where you can forgive
> And with each step that you try to take
> which alone can carry you a fantastic length
> let go of the thing known as "Foolish Pride."

Life, like driving, is a two-handed affair; it must be grasped firmly and taken seriously. Do not be fooled, great things are never stumbled upon. If you want to get anything meaningful out of life, you must add something meaningful to it. This requires your participation; constantly seeking pleasure is not the answer. Take the time to know yourself and have the courage to make the necessary hard decisions. The greater your goal, the greater the sacrifice will be. Simply ask yourself what you are prepared to give up to become the person you want to be. Remember, when preparation meets opportunity, the rest is history.

SPECIAL MENTION

I dedicate this portion of my book to my friends and well-wishers, to everyone who chose to share their thoughts and wisdom on what they believe the power of identity means. Thank you for sharing your thoughts. We have had many comments and have chosen these for publication.

The power of identity is crucial in the fact that we need to know who we are in order to understand our purpose in life. When we have no sense of the potential placed in us, we are unable to take steps to develop our God given abilities and talents. Once we have an understanding of whose we are and consequently who we are, we are empowered to dream and achieve acts beyond our wildest imagination.

—Tania Bogonko, Kenya

Coach Mwale understands that every person has fuel inside of them, to accomplish great things. Some people choose to leave the lid on however, in order to be great, you have to first know your identity. What is your God given identity?

—Doctor Cassama, Sweden

Who am I? Whose am I? Who will I become? Some crucial questions some may have figured out while the rest of us continue the search for answers. In most cases, we are given the opportunity to choose our careers, life partners, political and even religious affiliations which all add to the puzzle of our 'identity' or aid in our quest for self-understanding.

In every second, every minute and every hour of every day, it is important to understand who we are, whose we are, and who we will be so that we can live with determination for success and a hope for a more purposeful tomorrow.

—Naomi Richards, Trinidad

The power of identity encapsulates the courage of self to truly know, to love and to appreciate who you are. That is, to know you are ordained, equipped, positively purposeful and more than you ever dreamed of being. It gives you will power to overcome despite the odds, to choose the see the good in every situation and have an attitude of expectancy of nothing short of exceptional. It is one of our human super powers with no kryptonite.

—Reayah Francis, Tobago

The Power of Identity is an awesome topic for a book and discussion! I love Mwale & Chantel...they truly know how to inspire people. I remember being depressed for a month only to realize my self-identity needed healing. In this journey I was able to harness my ability to succeed

—Jeff Rahim Bronner, (Mayville, New York) USA

The financial life you have today is a result of choices you made & habits you formed over the years. But you don't have to continue in those habits. YOU CAN form new habits.

—Randy Bevins, (Ohio) USA

One's identity is what establishes the foundation for one's life. Out of what someone understands and accepts as their identity, comes their purpose, their worldview, what they will do, how they will do it and how they interact with the world itself. So in a sense, the identity that one takes unto himself/herself has the power to limit or encourage the quality of life that will be lived.

Acts 17:28 (NIV) **—Ebiakpo-aboere Sonron, Jamaica**

An individual's identity is created by the experiences he's had over his lifetime. The power of that identity, be it positive or negative, though it belongs to one person, has the potential to affect change in society and even the world. However, in order to harness the power of identity, one must answer the question…"Who am I?"

—Venus Pollard, Trinidad

The Power of my identity impacts my daily results. My daily results are a by product of:
1. What I know
2. Decisions I make
3. Actions I take
4. Sharing my actions so others can benefit

—Patrick Batty, (Toronto) Canada

As we are representatives of Excellence, we as game changers must make peace with our past so we can unreservedly dominate the future right now

—Gabriel Williams, Trinidad

Mwale Henry's book is one every young person should read. It will trigger in them the need to connect with the power which is embedded within them – the power which can be kept dormant by the negativities of the world we now live in – the power which should be released to impact others in a positive way... to be all we are called to be so that we can do all that we are called to do.

—Marion Herbertson, (Hampshire) United Kingdom

Power to do what you truly love and are called to do whether or not it is accompanied by the approval of others; Power to love and forgive others regardless of any wrongs they may have committed against you.

—Shannon Leacock, Barbados

Claim your FREE Gift at www.FaithTour.org

DID YOU KNOW?

The Power of Identity: 7 Steps to Overtake and Dominate is a Project of the non-profit organization: R.I.C.H Before 30 (RB3). RB3 was launched by Laptop Lifestyle, LLC which are both founded by Mwale Henry and Chantel Morant.

The RB3 movement is all about empowering 20-Somethings and Millennials to Reclaim their Independence and Create Hope for a better future.

We are a global network of young people who strive to positively impact the world through entrepreneurship and service.

While Coach Mwale is serving others in Finding their Abundant Increase This Hour; Coach Chantel is Helping Other People Excel.

F.A.I.T.H TOUR

Finding **A**bundant **I**ncrease **T**his **H**our

F.A.I.T.H on a Mission

Coach Mwale is traveling to Colleges, High Schools, Churches, and Community Centers throughout 6 countries sharing the message of F.A.I.T.H.

Young entrepreneurs, single parents, faith leaders and education practitioners are all asking for Coach Mwale!

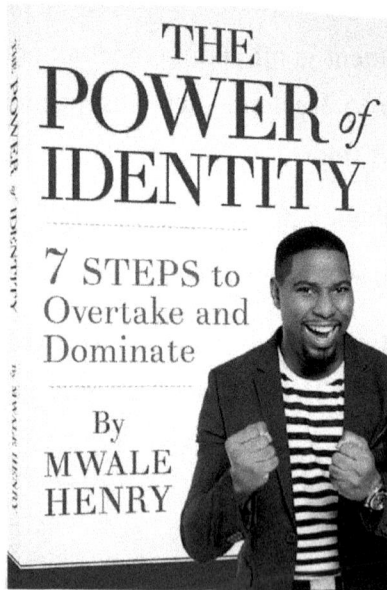

BOOK Coach Mwale for your next event!
www.coachmwale.com

Claim your FREE Gift at www.FaithTour.org

MISSION OF H.O.P.E. TOUR

Helping Other People Excel

Coach Chantel has embarked upon a 20-city Mission of H.O.P.E. Tour, to help high school juniors, seniors and college freshman, make college count!

On a Mission: 21 Secrets for College Success lays out easy-to-follow strategies for first-time college students to understand the right things to focus on to get better grades, stand-out from the competition while enjoying the best 4 years of their life!

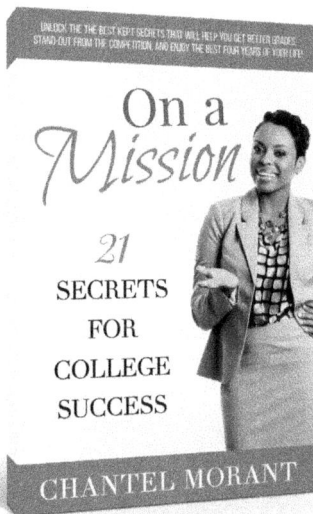

Get your copy TODAY!
www.chantelmorant.com

WORKS CITED

Quotes or Phrases in Book Inspired by the Bible and the Following:

Brown, Les. *Hard Times Go To Your Soul and Into Your Soul.* www.success.com/article/les-brown-hard-times-go-to-your-heart-and-into-your-soul. (Accessed January 5, 2015)

Cabrera, Angel. *Being Global: How to Think, Act, and Lead in a Transformed World.* Harvard Business Review Press: 2012.

Ecker, T. Harv. *Secrets of the Millionaire Mind.*

Jakes, Serita. www.christianpost.com/news/serita-jakes-on-how-to-help-insecure-girls-many-from-broken-families-feel-like-royalty-in-jesus-123412/ (Accessed January 6, 2015).

Jordan, Michael. Taken from www.complex.com/sports/2011/04/the-25-biggest-fails-in-nba-playoff-history/rasheed-wallace (Accessed January 2, 2015).

King Jr, Martin Luther. *The Class of Nonviolence: Loving Your Enemies.*

Gandhi, Mohamed. Taken from www.positivityblog.com/index.php/2008/05/09/gandhis-top-10-fundamentals-for-changing-the-world/ (Accessed January 5, 2015).

Gregory, Rebekah. *Rebekah Gregory DiMartino's New Day New Hope Facebook Page.* www.facebook.com/newday. newhope.rebekahgregory (Accessed January 2, 2015).

Maltese, Barry. *Forgiveness Poem.* 2000. Taken from www.crea8iv.com/forgiveness.htm (Accessed January 5, 2015)

Maraboli, Steve. Quotes taken from www.goodreads.com/author/quotes/4491185.Steve_Maraboli (Accessed January 5, 2015).

Marti, Jose. *I Have a White Rose to Tend.* Taken from www.allpoetry.com/I-Have-a-White-Rose-to-Tend-%28Verse-XXXIX%29 (Accessed January 7, 2015)

_____. *A Sincere Man Am I.* Taken from www.allpoetry.com/A-Sincere-Man-Am-I--%28Verse-I%29 (Accessed January 7, 2015).

Matty, Thomas. *You Can't be Anything You Want to Be.* Taken from www.thomasmatty.com/strengths/ (Accessed January 6, 2015).

ten Boom, Corrie. *The Hiding Place, 1971.*

Cubans Back TT Javelin Finalist. Trinidad and Tobago News-day, August 11, 2012. www.216.246.10.170/news/0,164619.html (Accessed January 2, 2015).

www.ingramcontent.com/pod-product-compliance
Lightning Source LLC
Chambersburg PA
CBHW072207090426
42740CB00012B/2428